Lea Utsira's

My Heart, Your Heart

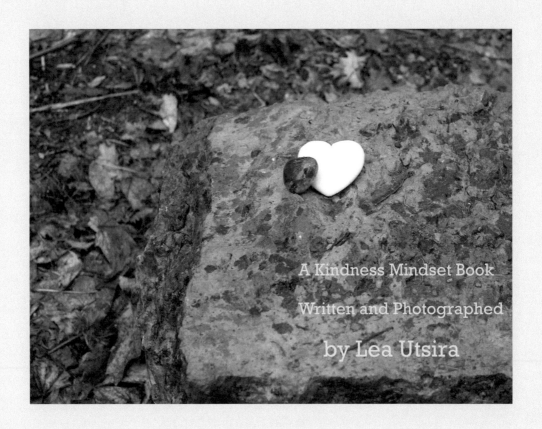

A Kindness Mindset Book

Written and Photographed

by Lea Utsira

My Heart, Your Heart

iUniverse books may be ordered through booksellers or by contacting:

iUniverse
1663 Liberty Drive
Bloomington, IN 47403
www.iuniverse.com
844-349-9409

ISBN: 978-1-6632-2192-6 (sc)
ISBN: 978-1-6632-2193-3 (e)

Library of Congress Control Number: 2021908483

Print information available on the last page.

iUniverse rev. date: 04/23/2021

My Heart, Your Heart

Your Heart

A Kindness Mindset Book

Written and Photographed

by Lea Utsira

This is a polished stone.

It is beautiful and special.

I held it in my hand, and felt it get warm.

I pressed it in my palms, then to my cheek, to remember the smoothness.

It is a garnet. I looked at it, and picked it up, every day.

I came on the long trip, then, and brought along the stone.

It was Autumn. I collected some leaves from outside, where they had turned yellow. I collected them after they fell.

Just like long ago, when I collected pretty leaves for Mother. I gave them to you, Mom, to see your smile.

My white stone stayed home. It was always my stone.

It is alabaster, carved to look like a Valentine.

It also warms up when I hold it in my hand. It is the twin of your garnet heart.

The garnet is shaped more like a real heart, beating inside your chest.

I found some moss to bring to you,
and we touched its softness. We
talked about the moss on my place,
and how I always brought moss
home, when I was little. You and I
would touch it back then, too. We
both loved Nature.

My alabaster heart reflects back the light, just like the moon. We share the moon. Find the moon, and think of me. I will find you in the moon, too.

I told you about the Half-Fallen Oak, on my place. You are old, but this Oak is much older. See how part of it has fallen? We thought and thought about that storm. It must have been a big one.

The mighty trunk is like us—like you and me. We have seen so much, and yet, we still stand.

Your heart has often been a light-hearted heart. Other old things, and toys, are fond of it.

It is important, when we are far away, to find the light-hearted little things.

We look for the light, the reflections of this world, as we live our closeness. We are lucky for our closeness, from near, or from far.

"Look! A tree floats in this water! Do you see? It is a blessing," we say to each other.

My heart found a place with friends, too.

Remember when I brought a frog inside, as a surprise, for you? I do!

Winter came, and we saw the the trees turn to frozen lace. Each in our own places now, we wrote to each other. We read good books, and talked about them. You told me that you read my letters five times. That made me smile, and I wrote more!

Remember our friend, Mevaline? We loved her so much. I named my Mevaline after her. There she is, with Dad's baby shoe. We always wondered, "What happened to the other shoe?"

Spring came, and I came to you again. I was so happy to hold your garnet, and make it warm for your hands. You tried to give it back to me. I said, "No! I have its twin. We can hold our stones and be close to each other."

My stone stayed back, and watched over the place. It shone like the moon, day and night. Find the moon, and think of me.

I will find you in the moon, too.

That last goodbye we had was so hard, but we were brave!

You still had your heart, and I had mine. We had the moon. The moon is ours, always.

I grew flowers for your butterflies. I sketched and painted and sent. You had them all over your little room!

So did I, in my outside rooms.

One day, I saw more than 25!

I thank you now, for them.

Today, our hearts are together again, at last. They live inside and outside. They visit and go back home, like I did.

The flowers grow, joyfully waiting for your butterflies. When I see them, I thank you. I know that when you see them, you smile somewhere, because love lasts forever.

My heart stays here, on your Memory Ledge,
most of the time. That is where I go to talk to you,
in peace and quiet. I know you are pleased
about this place. Love lasts forever.

I think you wanted me to write this book, so others will know how to do it, too! We can be glad for it.

Love lasts forever.

~Lorraine~

My mother and I celebrated the last year of her life here on Earth with letters, paintings, drawings, phone calls, and the two last big visits. That time was precious. In her 100 years of life, Lorraine gave love and joy to all who knew her, including her mother and sisters, pictured on the previous page. She is second from right, celebrating the peace that came that year.

I share the story of our twin heart stones, in hopes of helping others through the last shared time we are granted, with our loved ones.

From Lea Utsira~

I grew up in a big house in Madison, Wisconsin, and learned living in closeness, if near, or from far, from my parents, Richard and Lorraine. I taught Kindergarten, Pre-K and Early Grade Science in Brooklyn, New York, for many years. I grow lots of flowers, always keeping my eyes and ears open for the bees, birds and butterflies. Thanks to my readers! Remember to tread lightly in our natural world!

On the subject of mourning:

Finding notes, old letters, artifacts and other nostalgic things helps to deal with the deep feelings we are left with, after a death. I am blessed to have many photos and little things from my parents and grandparents. When I find a stone with an unusual shape, or see the Big Dipper, I always think of my father. When someone thanks me for a meal or a kind word, well spoken, my mother comes to mind.

Writing about the memories and their meanings is important, as we pass on the kindness, the essential core, of our loved one, to the next generation. I was once a bit afraid, when the feelings were less raw, less immediate, some months after my parents died. During the writing of My Heart, Your Heart, many deep, intense feelings came back to visit. This is the way of those who have loved. Love lasts forever. We feel, we love, we create meaning. Turn to Nature, and return this love. We bless their memories.

Lea Utsira

Printed in the United States
by Baker & Taylor Publisher Services